THE COSMIC BRAIN EXPLODES (A NEO-GNOSTIC TREATISE ON 'THE ETERNAL TRUTH')

Published by/Cyhoeddwyd gan Bardic
Press
Wesley House
Church Road
Cadoxton/Tregatwg
Barry/Y Barri
Vale of Glamorgan/Bro Morgannwg
Cymru

ISBN-13 978-1-906834-44-9

THE COSMIC BRAIN EXPLODES
(A NEO-GNOSTIC TREATISE
ON 'THE ETERNAL TRUTH')

MONTY OXYMORON

BARDIC PRESS
CADOXTON
2021

CONTENTS

ACKNOWLEDGEMENTS:

Here I must give thanks to and for that crazy conglomeration of beings that is my family: Diane, Francesca (my lovely creative sister), Julian and Ryan, thrown together into existence, founded on the rock that was my dear father J.W. Burrow who would surely be delighted that I am being incarnated in print on parchment; and to my uncle Damien Dunnington for lubricating my neural pathways with psychedelic juices from the Syd Barrett Floyd, Captain Beefheart, Jimi Hendrix, The Soft Machine... setting me forth on the strange sonic path to Damnation.

To my loving partner Kirsty Sloman for putting up with my madness and clutter for 25 years and keeping me in contact with sacred Nature.

And to my friends Henry Jaremko (who nourished my young Brain with the delights of Gong and Frank Zappa and who hosts and maintains my website); B12 Alasdair Willis (for opening ears to free jazz and experimental) and

Chris Mawer from that inexplicable Second Attic for encouraging me to keep playing through lockdown.

To the mysterious murmurings of Dr Space Toad, the flamboyant eruptions of Ian Smith (R.I.P.)

To the mesmerising manias of Mr Pottle the Tinram, and the Jazzticulations of Rod Paton of the Golden Horn.

To my dear friend Mr Daevid Allen who left us for 'the other side of the sky'; to Greene Johnny, Brian Zero and all of the family of Gong, and to the glorious god of Arthur Brown.

To that dysfunctional dynamism that is the Damned: we who build our very own Pandemonium, celebrate our marriage of Heaven and Hell, and then deconstruct the whole Phantasmagoria to move on elsewhere.

To the Vanian family and Aunty Jed, to pounding Pinch, throbbing Stu, and Paul Gray; to Joe De Lorenzo, Seano, and Martin of the sound.

And DEEP THANKS to the mighty Captain Sensible himself to whom I owe this splendid journey.

MONTY OXYMORON

To my American friends: Suzanne Ramsey (Kitten on the Keys) and Ward, to David Greenfield, Nancy Luna and Don Falcone in SF; and to the radiant inspirations of Ania Manicka, and Mo Russ for unleashing me on the East Coast.

To the staff and residents of Partridge House who seek to find and celebrate the light hidden within the occluding dark folds of dementia.

To Jay B. and all at Safehouse; to eccentric and irrepressible Roy; the Real Music Club and those Sumerian Kyngs.

To Pete Webster, Astrological Tim Burness, and Jem Hopkins for heady holistic pub and coffee conversations.

To the memory of Carolyn Marshall, whose journey into the underworld (and return) inspired my entry into nursing and transformed Douglas Adams' cosmic joke into a genuine search for the ultimate meaning of it all.

And also to Integral James Clifton for shining a light on the labyrinth of multiple perspectives and interesting me in Psychedelic therapy.

And finally with deep gratitude to my friend Andrew Phillip Smith for giving me this opportunity to release these inscriptions from the asylum of my brain.

FOREWORD

Those who have seen Monty Oxymoron on stage know him as a brilliant performer with a cartoonlike persona. Like one of the puppet musicians from the Muppet Show he combines frantic energy with his obvious love of playing, blending together the archetypes of mad scientist, nutty professor, nineteenth-century classical genius and cartoon punk. He stays in character throughout the gig, whether pogoing on the spot behind his keyboards during the guitar-based earlier numbers, whirling away from his instrument in a 360 degree turn that that lands his fingers back on the keyboard in exactly the right place, a little Richard re-made middle-aged Englishman, raising his arms in evangelic piety during 'Antipope', culminating in the mad dance that he performs centre-stage at some point in every Damned gig.

Yet the swirling arpeggios that he improvises prior to some appearances of the Damned are one indication that Monty is deeply intelligent. I first encountered Monty in the flesh backstage at the Academy in Dublin when he put me on the guest list. He had contacted me having read my book on the Gnostics (for which he wrote a foreword when it went into a second edition as *Secret History of the Gnostics*). I discovered that Monty was a sincere seeker after things that were higher (or deeper, depending on your spatial metaphor.)

The work you hold in your hand, *The Cosmic Brain Explodes*, was written as a stream of consciousness piece. Monty is at pains to tell us that this stream of consciousness was not caused by an altered state of consciousness, either of pharmaceutical or spiritual origin.

On the Eternal Truth is influenced by Monty's wide reading of and exploration in spiritual traditions. References to William Blake and the Sufis, to Jung and new physics may be discerned. But overall the flavour and the language of the work is Gnostic.

For anyone unfamiliar with the concept, Gnosticism is a tradition that goes back at least to the early centuries of our era. Yes, it emphasises spiritual seeking but often flips conventional interpretations on their heads.

It may posit an intangible and remote original spiritual origin to the world, but for Gnostics the conventional forms of religion are often seen as worshipping the wrong figure—a false creator God who is concerned with keeping mankind under his thumb, weighed down by the basic difficulties of living in a material world, numbed into a condition of ignorance and forgetfulness, asleep to our real possibilities. Monty uses the language and themes of Gnosticism in a way that is authentic to the original sources yet is entirely individual.

Monty asked me to rearrange the components of the writing, to bring out themes and variations as did T.S. Eliot in *Four Quartets*. This proved a greater challenge than I expected and I ended up printing out the whole thing, cutting it into separate paragraphs and spreading these out and shuffling and rearranging them on our living room carpet until I came up with an arrangement that we were both happy with. The cover and interior images are also by Monty. Their cosmic and psychedelic style and themes mirror Monty's music and writing.

Monty is not a navel-gazer. Aside from his music he is a psychiatric nurse dealing with mostly elderly dementia patients. He cares for others and gives care.

The Cosmic Brain Explodes offers a voice—in fact, more than one voice. It questions, it offers a Gnostic diatribe. Humour is never too far away. Anyone who is interested either in Monty or in Gnosticism will be surprised and engaged by his Gnosis.

Andrew Phillip Smith

Introduction:

In the mid-1980s I was training to become a psychiatric nurse at Graylingwell hospital, one of the old mental asylums now being converted into housing. One day I found myself, a rather shy student nurse, in the office of one the 'acute' wards; that is one dealing with new admissions. In those days we were crammed into a small office full of smoke (before the ban of more enlightened times) when a woman I hadn't seen before burst into the room unannounced and said, 'There will be seven writers who will write a book on the Eternal Truth... and you're one of them!' pointing straight at me. At the time I'd been reading a lot of C.G. Jung's work and so I replied: 'Oh... seven evangelists this time?' (to the obvious surprise of the nurses.)

'That's it: you've got it!' she answered and left.

It's often been women who have inspired me in life's directions. For example, when I was a young boy I used to visit a woman who travelled in visionary landscapes and created pictures of them: nature spirits, multicoloured skies and amazing buildings lined with sculptures of hollowed out lions filled with honey. This later inspired both my interest in spiritual art (such as Blake's) and in art therapy: the sharing of creativity and inner intimacy. To such 'Beatrices' I dedicate my 'Hymn to Sophia': the Goddess of Wisdom in remembrance of the fact that a philosopher is always 'a lover of Wisdom'.

I'd forgotten about this Sophianic encounter until years later when I was writing up memories. Since then I'd been introduced, mainly by Jung, to the ancient Gnostics. Knowing that they were fond of creating their own gospels and other speculative writings, I thought 'Well why not try and do just that?'

So I began writing whenever the impulse took me in a small purple book that I kept by my bedside for several years. I allowed the thoughts and feelings to flow freely without judgement or censor: I was surprised at what was emerging.

In addition to those ancient Gnostics I'd become aware of many other esoteric traditions especially that of the Islamic mystics so beautifully introduced in the works of Henry Corbin, and also the Sufis. Also in the mix were the modern scientific theories and concepts that have uprooted and challenged our assumptions about reality. If that wasn't enough, poststructuralist and postmodernist attacks on the very notion of a metaphysical 'truth' were also lubricating the synapses.

In that context 'The Eternal Truth' would seem an imperialist concept reeking of metaphysics and thus ripe for deconstruction. However in *Trump and a Post-Truth World* (Shambhala Publications Inc, 2017) integralist philosopher Ken Wilber argues passionately that in banishing truth itself postmodernist thought unwittingly created an ideological vacuum in which any narcissist can claim that, 'Truth is what I want it to be and say it is!" We know well that scientists subject their theories to 'falsification', and that if the theory survives that treatment it is more likely to be considered true. But how many of us subject our emotional, psychological, political and aesthetic 'theories' to such a test? Surely these 'truths' are equally important, especially if we want to avoid the narcissism Wilbur describes. Why is it we are so keen to embrace some memes, allow them to lodge in our psyche, define ourselves by them and shout about them on social media? 'We are all Ego Warriors', according to Neil Innes! 'Truth' then becomes inseparable from 'belief' (Pistis rather then Gnosis.)

It seems to me that we are inundated with too many 'truths': too much information/misinformation, lies and rumours of lies, part truths, distortions and delusions. You can take your pick from the various conspiracy theories, dangerous memes and fiercely held dogmas and create your own canon of rigid opinions, and thus shackle your-self with 'Mind Forged Manacles.'

Memes apart, an unpleasant fact we all need to face is that we are cer-tainly ruining the planet we depend and live upon and that is so regard-less of whether or not one believes in manmade climate change. Deconstruct that one and we will all find ourselves homeless in the cosmos.

Of course the postmodern decon-struction of truth is rooted in a reac-tion to the tendency to dogma that has enslaved our thinking over and over throughout history but, as Wilber sug-gests, it has led to a new 'slavery', the grip of nihilism and narcissism that paralyses thought even more than dogma. The Gnostics and the Sufis managed to retain a freedom of thought and spirit right in the very midst of such dogma and many were persecuted and killed for doing so. For them there is indeed a wider higher realm of Truth that transcends all our bewildering array of opinions considered as facts that is rooted in a direct spiritual experience that cannot be tested, measured or even directly described.

However, the writings of postmodernists are not merely nihilistic and Wilber suggests we 'include' their insights rather than banish them. They are often complex, apophatic and paradoxical: qualities they share with the Gnostic texts I have been reading and enjoying. The influence of experimental literature such as that of James Joyce and Gertrude Stein also have their place in attempts to think the unthinkable and express the inexpressible.

Thus In the spirit also of the Surrealists I deliberately set out to write as automatically as possible; to set aside the critical part of the mind and allow the ideas to flow whereever they wished to go. This little text is the result. As I was reading Wilber I also reacquainted myself with a Traditional Sufi story told by Idries Shah in his *Thinkers of the East* entitled 'The Land Of Truth' (Penguin Books, 1971, pages 66-67.) In that story it is suggested that both Happiness and Misery can imprison us while, as has been said, 'The truth will set you free.' I found myself as a child to be suspended between two polarised world views (as we all seem to be these days.) My mother, a very creative and imaginative woman, is a devout and enthusiastic promotor of an exoteric literal interpretation of the Bible, whereas my father, J.W. Burrow, a well-known intellectual historian was of the atheist persuasion. I was never happy with either of those extremes so what does that make me but an Oxymoron! I searched and read and thus found my way to the spiritual mavericks, the heretics and mystics.

The text itself, as you will see, seldom refers to truth directly: its presence is there, like the proverbial 'elephant in the room', yet the room is in darkness and the presence is touched gently rather than grasped. Multiple perspectives rearrange themselves from different angles like the images produced in early cubism: 'But you can't see what it is!' Indeed what it is remains elusive. In science it is that which cannot be disproved, while in our social and political life it becomes problematic: search engines guide us to opinions presented as factual expressed in a violent intrusive and dominant way, with desperation as if to try and reinstate dogmatic assumptions and exclude all dissent. Meanwhile a more transcendent truth becomes still more elusive than the 'accurate and complete information' we so badly need to make sense of our confusing world. Maybe painting, architecture or music may come closer to this, but here we are in the realm of words. Language tends to imprison us in its dualistic grammatical schema; yet poetry has been able to stretch it to describe and point to the ineffable. So we must try…

The great question: 'What is truth?' is met with a deafening silence in the New Testament and so here are my tentative meandering musings on the matter. Our truth may well die with us but the Eternal Truth will continue and may in time be rediscovered by other seemingly intelligent beings, either here on Earth,... or elsewhere. (I'm very much looking forward to meeting and working with the other six writers.)

Monty Oxymoron 2018-2021.

THE COSMIC BRAIN EXPLODES
(A NEO-GNOSTIC TREATISE
ON 'THE ETERNAL TRUTH')

HYMN TO SOPHIA

To She

To She who Is

To She who is Wisdom,
Implicit without knowing it.
She who saw the invisible worlds
And revealed them in images.
She who descended into the
   Underworld
And returned with the Light
She who was wounded and yet healed
She whose heart beats to Nature's
   rhythm
Who is a warrior AND who nurtures life
She whose very presence is Visible
   Music
Radiating love to all people
She who saves animals
And whose eyes are full of infinite Love

Oh Sophia, Goddess of Wisdom
Teach me, Inspire me
To ever greater and further things.

I

1
'I'

'In the names of the Creative, the Transcending, the Imaginal... '

'I am in the before,'

'I am pre-beginning. Before the Word, before the Thought, before Knowledge.'

'In the infinitely small seed of potentiality I sing silently; I breathe my own being timelessly.'

'From where you are now I cannot be: there is no place for the before there, no space in the before in which I or anything can be... yet I am there. '

'Not 'was' as there is yet no time: can the before be in the now? In the process: the non-process; the before process. Infinite process mirrors infinite regress, yet the process is not yet.'

'I am "the hidden treasure that wishes to be known," yet I can only be known if there are knowers; I can only be known in knowers, in their knowing of themselves in that I can know myself knowing them in me. Therefore here must I begin... '

'In a sense I end here: I empty myself of all singularity, of all sufficiency, of all fullness. I surrender all I am outwardly into the new fullness, the ever expanding Pleroma of the All, into a new multitude of forms ever appearing. I become nothing to allow the All to become, that I might come to be in the All.'

'I explode with creation and destruction, ever more, ever further. Endless swirls of complexity pour from me ever outward until the non-me comes to be that in which I can be born.'

2
THE EMERGING

From singularity comes forth duality: light and dark, hot and cold, movement and stillness. Then triangularities, quaternities, multiple qualities endlessly dancing and multiplying. Fragments and wholes, strands and swirls, arabesques and curls; ever changing calligraphic fractals of light and colour: the 'writing' of the Pleroma, its signatures: ever more, ever further.

Messages embedded not in the chemistry, the energy or even in the light. Not in the tiny forces and spectral forms. Not in the vast shapes and galactic dances, nor even in the numbers. The meanings are in the patterning, in the fullness' self-organising: ever more, ever further. Until it is self-shaped into crystalline forms that finally weave themselves into living things: the knowing is then in the life, in the life is the knowing.

There is but one flesh of the whole world: one ever changing, forming, re-forming field of flesh. All feeling, moving, stretching, seeing, smelling, reaching, touching, hearing together. The flesh of being continually eats, kills and gives birth to itself. A labyrinthine mesh of experiencing living changing, expanding, contracting connectivity. Wherever it can become it will form. Wherever it can stretch and seed itself it will extend. Its inner 'intelligence' is seemingly unstoppable though it appears weak and fragile. And even as it appears the space changes to hold it for the universes are indeed pregnant with life.

And as the space is pregnant with life so life is pregnant with consciousness, and in turn consciousness is pregnant with that for which it came into being.

3
BIRTH OF THE DEMI-EGO

And so consciousness came to be, but instead of emptying itself into the Pleroma ever more it fell in love with its own image in matter: 'I am the Telos of creation, there is nothing greater than I!' 'I am Alpha and Omega, I am God and no one else!' But then, unable to empty itself it senses isolation and becomes afraid. Being fearful it divides the world into pain and pleasure, good and evil, friend and foe, same and different. Then it seeks to control define and separate all things through laws, threats, punishments and rewards. It splits itself into 'us' and 'them', 'Me' and 'other'. Becoming inharmonious with conditions it finds scarcity, unreliability and poverty in the world. It retreats further demanding all good for 'Me' 'Mine' and 'Ours' and all badness for 'the other' and 'them'. And thus hate is born in the universe and with it ignorance, greed and small mindedness. Looking upwards it sees itself mirrored in the sky, distorted with wrath and vengeance. Sometimes it forgets itself and fears its own image there, and the hate that is really its own projected thus.

4
The Highest Thought

Eternity is in love with the productions of time'[1]: and so what manifestations are found in the world of the limited, the temporary, and the temporal? What you look for you find, what you believe in you imagine, what you imagine you create, and what you create finds you. So be careful!

An anguished voice calls out:

'Oh you who shape my being thus!'

'You have made me into stars, into mountains, rivers, seas.'

'You have made me into plants, animals.'

'You have made me into woman and man, and mixtures of the human and the bestial forms.'

'I empty myself: whatever you wish for I will become, whatever you seek you will find, whatever seed you sew will grow for you. Your voice goes forth, and the echo returns to you.'

'So why, why do you mould me into hateful, ugly and wrathful forms? Why must I become abusive, unforgiving, the un-merciful, the un-compassionate, insecure, jealous, megalomaniac, rigid? Seek for my expansiveness, forgiving, Mercy, Compassion, Beauty. Call on THESE names: all this I can be, and more, to those who see aright.'

'Yet beyond this, the wiser still empty themselves as I empty myself, into the Fullness: these allow me to Be. Without expectations, without reward or punishment. Without preconception, without prejudice, without even belief! To allow me to Be: whatever I shall be to that one. Those are so rare!'

'I am abused every day, and being abused I abuse through the abusive who abuse in my names! You ask me endlessly for mercy, but when will you have mercy toward me? So much so that I feel relief when you refuse all belief, hope and imagining: then comes the relief of my being nothing... if that is your wish.'

'But know then you are alone: tiny and short lived in the vastness of the Fullness: it could be so different!'

5
EPIPHANY

The sacred is hidden, occulted in the profane. The significant is hidden in the mundane. When all things come together in significant harmony, then what occurs is 'just right': in place like a particular note in a musical piece's trajectory and is effective. Know then that perfection and beauty have come to touch this world before returning to their own place. Everyone strives for perfection (often without knowing it); for the manifestation of its epiphany. It IS real, even here and now... but only briefly, subtly, diaphanous and fleeting, light and swift. So catch it, experience it, and joy in it while it is there!

And when it's gone: remember it!

II

1
KENOMA

Kenoma: thick impenetrable swathes of dark gloom. Where now is the inspiration; where is the knowledge; where the light? The fullness is now dim and distant. Outwardly life is successful: inwardly all is chaos and poverty! The tiniest of things stirs the mind into swirls of misunderstanding and fear unbounded. The maelstrom of indignation, the hoping for the impossible, the ridicule of all attainment, possibility, realisation. The victory of the futile, the unworthy; the bitter poisonous sclerosis of the mind. Endless a-gnosis and a-pistis appear. The oozing mud of mundanity encloses over the head and occludes the airways choking inspiration before it can enter.

Seemingly, without result I seek within and without. I scour texts of the whole world for wisdom. The wisest words: 'When death comes not one phrase of it will be of any use!'

2
REALISATION OF THE DEMI-EGO

One great voice was heard: 'All I have made is flawed, is wrong, and broken: for all my power I myself am in need of a higher realisation. I seek redemption for myself and all I have made in my power. Those who know will be of service to this end.'

'Awaken: small temporary flesh. Awaken: tiny drop of liquid. Awaken: little sigh of breath. Awaken: quiet murmur, voice unheard. Awaken: little mind, unknown, unknowing.'

'Know yourself to be the All: the totality of the Pleroma.'

'My flesh, my bones are of the one great Earth. My fluid, ancient oceans. My breath is of the winds: the breathing of the world. My voice: the universal sound and my thought is of the one great thought.'

'As there is only one great life, so too there is only one death. Let my silent breath be that of before the before and after the afterward, that all will exist in eternity… after all physical breath is no more…'

3
THE MISSING PART

He... is missing from the universe: the sign on the door of the temple said: 'He is not in here!'[5] So maybe the missing portion of the universe is itself He. No sign, no loud voice, no grand display in physis, only the what is, the visible, the revealed. Not visible in the world of the very tiny (where humans peer and dabble), nor in the world of the unimaginable vastness is He seen. Only here do we hear talk of Him, of the world as His artefact. Is He then not? Or could it be that in order for the All to be, He made himself empty and even absent: the ultimate Kenosis! Emptied Himself so that we could be. Then in turn we can empty ourselves of self, and allow Him to be, to impossibly give birth, like the virgin to Him. When we merge as Nous: the Mind of the All, we can know ourselves as He. Then the tail of the serpent is in its mouth and the circle is completed and our minds are squared. Thus His non-being becomes

Being in our non-being: the whole pageant, the phantasmagorical play of the world reveals its purpose and culmination.

All having been said before, all that remains to say is 'Beyond the beyond, there is an All and everything that knows; and its knowing knows no ending... '

4
PLEROMA: LOVE, BEAUTY, TRUTH

God is one, but is also the many. The Pleroma is the fullness of manifestations: all thoughts in one thought, each thought in the all. They have a trinity: Father, Son, Spirit; you too have a trinity: Truth, Love, Beauty. To know true reality you must realise what these three are and what they really mean.

To doubt these is to destroy spirit; to explain them in terms of the mundane is to dilute them. All ask 'is there a God?' Would you ask also: is there truth, is there love, is there beauty? Truth seems harsh and exacting while love is the mediator. Yet love also demands: honesty, searching, devotion and faith. Beauty is the essence of manifestation: beauty touches the world and then withdraws to its own place. Happy is the one who makes the way to the domain of beauty! For there beauty remains always.

MONTY OXYMORON

And now the transformation is for real, and for the Real. All must be placed on the line for the All. That which is most feared must be faced, and that which is held on to must be let go. What once was virtue may be recognised as slavery, as a chain that binds us to the darkness.

That poet's guidance: to read scripture 'in its infernal aspect'[4]; the Gnostic twist: to reverse the endorsements, these turn the inward upside down; inside out; back to front in order that the meaning may cast off its burden and reveal the juice of the innermost meaning.

Mirroring the literal left to right 'God is love' becomes 'Love is God': to find the true love is to find God, and the path is just as arduous. Faith and doubt will fight; hope and despair will dance together wildly. Real agony and ecstasy will appear in equal terns, until the real vision sings truly.

Man has killed God, dismantled faith, and abolished the soul: yet many still believe in love, beauty and truth. As ideas if not as experiences; if not here in life, then elsewhere. To find these is to find, realise, and create God: then in turn God finds, realises, and creates Being in and through our finding, realising and creating.

An echo of the absolute returns to us through the shadows and mist of our doubt, our impotence and our heedlessness. The great battle, the war of light and darkness from the beginning to the ending, takes place in the individual soul. We are suspended in mid-air between oppositions: in our success the victory of light, life and good is realised. The burden is heavy, the balance critical, the 'trust' is real... but we are destined to succeed! This is when body becomes pure spirit and the resurrection takes place!

III

1
SOMETHING MORE

Is the universe incomplete? Would we know if it was? And how? Maybe by our hankering after 'something' and our yearning for 'something more'. We have become suspicious of our meta-narratives; so why have we created them, what purpose have they served for us all this time? Is part of the universe missing? How much; half... two thirds? We know of and by physics: the body, the 'stuff' of the world Matter; the body: all explained, fixed, certain, reduced to the idea fully defined, examined, described and measured in detail.

Once there were two additional worlds: those of spirit and soul. We wonder at the vision of the world: why need we imagine phantoms at the edge of the limits of our intrusion? Why indeed? Why ghosts, spirits, demons and gods when humans can fulfil and live all these parts in the play of being? Why indeed? For our ancestors the world of Spirit was 'the Real': ours was the illusion. In between the two the realm of soul existed with its own concerns, inhabitants and happenings.

So if the universe is incomplete indeed, most of it is hidden from us.

2
Thoughts of The Demi-Ego

Away with the old books! Away with the tomes full of curses that bind! Away with the old god of the ignorant and the blind! That Great Terrorist who governs by means of endless threats and promises.

Like a child with a big drum He raises a foolish din: 'I am God and there is no other! I will enslave all minds by means of fear and longing. With unbreakable chains of guilt I will weigh them down into the pit! With shame born of their innermost obsessions and dreams I shall imprison them! So that they might praise Me, for I need praise and sacrifice and rulership and dominion! Attend to Me: to the thunder of my big drum, and tremble, for I know your innermost thoughts, feelings and desires; your dread, your shamefulness, regret, wastefulness and sorrow!'

The ignorant are thus bound to even kill and be killed in His names. Thus it is written in the Book of Curses, the

Book of Condemnation and the Chronicles of Hate! That heavy law and 'Truth' that makes a chain gang of all peoples. The heavy letters of the Law hewn in stone, set in branding iron and burning lead!

There is a new scripture: but it is not this... NOT THIS! Not in ink on page or parchment, not in black dots and lines in front of our eyes. It is inscribed with invisible hands on the tissues of the soul. THIS is true knowledge: the Gnosis of the ultimate. Men think knowledge is in information: they collect millions of facts, ideas and ideas of ideas: mounds of thought pile up like books on rubbish tips, all thick and black with writing. But facts are like flotsam and jetsam: small poisoning motes thrown up at the edge of the sea of being. Information is that grey film of slime on its surface.

Gnosis is that unfathomable sea itself...

3
TRUTH IS TOO CLOSE!

Truth is 'closer than your jugular vein.'[2] Closer than the eyeball to its sight. Closer than ears to sound: so I can't see nor hear it. Closer than touch to my fingers, so I can't grasp it. Closer than my taste buds so I can't savour its juices. Closer even than my very nerve cells so I cannot think it.

Oh Truth, you are too close! Retreat please: make some distance. Open a space between us, a space in which I may see you. A gap through which I may hear you. The surface of a barrier: an edge that I may touch! Then you can be 'other' that I may get to know you...

... so strange! I want you as near as, but am forced to push you away: be far!

Be near! In your distance be most near! Then I can hear the essence of 'another' on the far side of me. I see the edges of your being only. I can only touch what is separate from me: what misery! I join my hands in prayer because I want: NO SEPARATION!

May I find new perceptive organs requiring no separation in order to know. May I find a new mind not imprisoned in this tiny skull and its small apertures that let in some light! Show me the way out of my cave prison: could I but see Truth as me, and me as nothing... but Truth.

4
THE MANIFESTATION

'Before the beginning I am in the realm of pure perfection: I am all and nothing. Absent of qualities and distinctions, I am free of phenomena. I am at peace in my oneness.'

'I am silent. Shining in pure light I am at rest in darkest night. I am.'

'No birth, no death; no beginning, no end. No meeting, no parting. No colours, no forms; no pleasure, no pain. Complete in dreamless sleep in eternity: a hidden treasure. So whence comes this wish to be known? I wish... to be known in a new way. I will become therefore. I will take on forms that I may know those forms in myself.'

'Some pulse: some urge stretches me forth: a need to grow, to change, and to stretch myself out into the world as living expanding entities. I reach into the sky and grasp the sunlight: I reach into the moist earth and anchor myself.'

'A spark across the threshold, a pulse across the abyss: I become animal. I move and breathe; I reproduce, am born, give birth and, yes, die. I will know what textures, smells, tastes, colours, pleasure and pain are. I take on endlessly varied numerous forms (beautiful, ugly, strange, ridiculous and fantastic) as I spread abroad.'

'Once again the spark flies across the gap and I become... human. In this form I will manifest mind so that I may become aware of all of my manifestations. A few, (but only a few), will come to know themselves as me... in them.'

'But this is but another resting place, another oasis on the journey: that spark will cross again and again to produce other unimaginable forms. But in the human form I grow weary. I know division, hate and conflict. I know violence. I know despair, ennui, longing and disappointment, disillusion and oppression. In the human I forget who I am!'

'Thus I must seek myself in this endless display, until I find myself. Finding myself I am still troubled and astonished. But then I will find rest and at last rule over all the forms in which I previously manifested. Then I will know myself in my fullness.'

'Then all will be complete.'

IV

1
THE MADNESS

The Pleroma... is coming! The fullness that is hidden in the minds of all who think. It is the fullness of Mind itself and is potentially omnipresent. Let the minds crack open so its nectar may be revealed! The thought that is in all lives at all times and in every place: it will emerge! Those that know are truly free of the chains and manacles of time and space: they leap like sparks form mind to mind, from life to life, through the galaxies, indeed the universes forever!

Let the knowing then be known; let all thought be free that the All may Be: All in All. The Pleroma is coming... and it is here!

Let ignorance end, and death and non-life cease; let the galaxies be living beings and each star a light of thought in a single mind: the Mind of the All!

In a vast temple bigger than all the temples of the world ever built I hear the sound of a thousand struck strings, a thousand thousands! In the earth-quake of sound, the sound of all sounds is released – a roaring torrent of the noise of the Cosmos floods all thought with power. That power swells and builds and breaks its bounds beyond all enduring. Montanus Doxomedon[3] has heard it. Now it must be incarnated in all ears.

Break open the bones and let loose their marrow: break open the shell and find the pearl; the kernel, indeed the kernel of the kernel to reveal the inner meanings. Cast aside the husk of literal meanings in the sacred texts and utterances. The 'marrow of Gnosis' is hidden in the inside of the inside.

2
THE DEMI-EGO REPENTS

'I was unaware, I was unconscious of my creative faculty: thus I am not evil, I intend no harm. Unaware my passions, my thoughts and dreams gave birth to beings in my interior worlds and I, languishing in the mists of my aloneness caused them to come forth from the depths of my sorrow.'

'My tears became floods and tidal storms that swept them away but I knew it not. My great anger and frustration brought forth earthquakes, eruptions, violent hurricanes and devastation, but I knew it not. My long sadness descended upon them with thick endless grey clouds obscuring their sun... and I knew it not!'

'Finally the light from above shone into my being: I awoke to their cries, to their torment and I resolved to refresh and renew my domains with joy, love and creative power that the sun might shine on them once more.'

So beware then: those climates and weather of the mind: inners doubt, anguish and terror may create misery for the inhabitants of your own inner kingdom. Enrich those beings with your love, your goodness, your strength. Know that all here are in need of great enlightenment, illumination and refreshment of mind, from those who appear small and unworthy to those who appear most great in this life: may they all attain!

3
REVEALING MIND EQUALS TRUTH

You have heard no doubt, of the spirit in the bottle; of the prisoners in the cave who see only shadows. The skull is the bottle and the cave. Release the spirit from the bottle: the prisoners from the gilded cage!

'I have split open the stick of myself and lifted up my own grave stone, and I go from resurrection to resurrection. In the light of the new scripture written on my heart all doors open to me, all doorkeepers stand aside. I, Montanus Doxomedon, cross over the world as a bridge and to the limitless splendour I make my way that the true fulfilment of being may be revealed through the All and in the All.'

The one that walks will still walk, and live, and eat and earn as well as all other mundane things: but all is transformed! The prison into a palace: the felon, a king.

Split apart the atom of yourself and the energy will erupt from within. But this explosive power neither destroys nor maims, but unfolds itself unto endless intricate forms of meaning dancing into life with endless novelty and complexity. Everything dances, everything sings, everything means and lives with the golden cry: 'UNIVERSE, UNIVERSE, UNIVERSE!'

One life in all lives; one thought in all thoughts, one mind alive with love and joy.

When the seals of the mind are broken and what is revealed are no longer curses, laws, penalties, bribes and empty promises. The living truth of ancient Gnosis bursts through, ever new, ever alive: a great tidal wave of meanings washes away ignorance and small mindedness.

Now, here and always bathe and be baptised into the foam of meanings, and the meaning of meanings and be renewed, released, revived!

Here ends the Oxymoron Codex!

NOTES:

1. William Blake.

2. Attributed to Mohammad and often quoted by the Sufi mystics.

3. 'Montanus Doxomedon'. The name I take on here is an amalgamation of two names (chosen loosely on the basis that it resembles my stage name). Firstly Montanus was an ecstatic self-proclaimed prophet who said: 'Behold man is as a lyre and I play upon him as with a plectrum, man sleeps and I arouse him, it is the Lord who throws men's souls into ecstasy and gives them a heart.'(*Encyclopaedia of Heresies and Heretics*, Chas S. Clifton, ABC-CLIO Inc., 1992, p98.) He lived in the first century and his church elevated women to high office. (*A Dictionary of Gnosticism*, Andrew Phillip Smith, Theosophical Publishing House, 2009, p164) Domedon Doxomedon is a spirit being: the 'Aeon of Aeons' and 'Lord of the House' who appears in a number of

Gnostic texts. (Ibid p73.) So this composite identity (and entity) represents a pretty megalomaniac identification. In a note by this portion of the text I wrote: 'Self-delusion, close to madness!' I kept it in as I wanted to maintain the free-flow of thought. (If like Nietzsche, who signed his letters 'Yours, Dionysus Zagreus' I start to refer to myself thus, then I may need returning to the place that initiated this piece of work.)

4. William Blake.

5. I say 'He' here as in traditional Sufi literature, but one could equally say 'She': the Goddess. 'And even more so neither He nor She, is God an it? Is God an it? Is God in it? That is all I ask before I quench my thirst, unhinge my heart, drench my soul' ('Non God Will Not Go On', Daevid Allen, 'Daevid Allen N'existepas!', Charley Records, 1979.)

Notes on the Images:

Front cover: 'Implicit Text' Monty Oxymoron, digital art.

1. 'Brain-Tree-Dark-Sun' Monty Oxymoron, pen and ink.

Sitting under an apple tree in meditation during 'the season of apples' under the full moon as prescribed in Robert Graves' *The White Goddess* in search of wisdom. It was 2012 and a week later I speak of this to Daevid. 'Well, whatever it IS it will make is WORSE', he said with a grin, and added 'That's the whole point!' The first of two tree images in this book: the association between trees, thought and knowledge, is an ancient one. The 'Arbor Vitae' resides in the cerebellum: does it have hidden properties we have forgotten? Trees branch ever outward creating complex patterns in the air as they reach toward capturing the source of energy in their leaves and produce the fruitage we can eat. In our minds this produces resonance creating inner calm. In our brains too the neurons 'branch out' forging new connections and pathways of thought, feeling and sense. These too we hope will be fruitful!

At the centre of the 'tree brain': the 'Sol Niger' of the alchemists, their 'Prima Materia'. Therein the Thalamus, the 'Bridal Chamber'. Physically the Thalamus unites the forces of the sympathetic and the parasympathetic, activity and rest, 'movement and repose'. Could it be the place of the wedding between the two incompatible worlds of the right and the left hemispheres so gloriously described in Iain McGilchrist's majestic opus *The Master and His Emissary*? The Gnostic marriage of Soul and Spirit, the Valentinian union of Mind and Truth, of the Conscious and the Unconscious in the work of C.G. Jung take place there in the dark Latifa of the Sufi. (See *The Master and his Emissary: The Divided brain and the Making of the Western World*, Iain McGilchrist, Yale University Press, 2009. *A Dictionary of Gnosticism*, Andrew Phillip Smith, Quest Books 2009, p49; *Gnosticism, Its History and*

Influence, Benjamin Walker, Crucible, 1989, p123.) Some say the Thalamus is the legendary 'Third Eye'.

2. 'The Distorted Mirror in the Sky', pen and ink.

'Looking upwards it sees itself mirrored in the sky, distorted with wrath and vengeance. Sometimes it forgets itself and fears its own image there, and the hate that is really its own projected thus.' A reversal of the natural correspondence 'As above, so below', here 'As below, so above, as within, so without': our own darkness becomes the image of worship, fear and trembling. Should our gods and goddesses not rather be images of beauty, love and forgiveness to inspire us to be more, and better than we are rather than worse? We are responsible!

3. 'The Crowned Fish', pen and ink.

I think it was 1990, I was attending a weekend workshop at Hawkwood College in Stroud that brought together art, music, dance and enactment as therapies. Joy Schavarien, the Jungian art psychotherapist was running the art group and Robert Hobson (who knew Jung personally), ran the enactment group. At the end we showed each other's groups the fruits of our labours: ours was the exhibition of the art. In it I had drawn the image of a fish with wings and legs breathing fire to represent the Symbol as a union of opposites as spoken about in Mr Hobson's opening address. When I had finished it a 'voice' (I didn't physically hear it, but felt it) said quite clearly: 'Stick a crown on it!' So straight away I did with a blue crayon. At the exhibition someone exclaimed: Robert's got to see this!' He came over and shook my hand warmly. While we were working hidden from us in another room in that magical house, the enactment group were busy miming and visualising: their theme: The Fisher King!

4. 'The Oxy-Tree' , pen and ink.
Among my childhood drawings there is one that features a tree with wings. I

was using this to represent renewal and the restoration of paradise (the Arbor Vitae again!) Years later it seemed to me a good image of the paradox that we are:

'I can't possibly be what I am

I can't possibly be what I'm not

I can possibly be what I can't possibly be;

So let's see what on earth I have got!'

As Oscar Wilde said as we lie in the gutter some of us gaze upward. We are rooted in our bodies and to the earth, thoroughly 'earthbound'. This is may be no bad thing as our embodiment itself produces the enrichment of our daily experience and relationships. Yet with our curiosity, inventiveness and imagination we soar far into the depths of space and time. While our scientists use technology to probe deep into space with astonishing results, mystics and visionaries travel with their expanded faculties into the heights and depths of imaginal inner worlds.

The human condition is one of paradox and we are all an oxymoron... like a tree with wings!

Laurence Burrow came into existence in September 1961 in Cambridge England. In 1969 the family moved to Hove when his father J.W. Burrow started lecturing at Sussex University and, apart from studying in Chichester, he has lived in the Brighton area ever since. His main interests lay in the area of art and music originally. (Laurence's uncle Damien Dunnington, creator of pirate radio station 'Radio Ginger' in Cambridge had made him aware of the music of the counter culture when he was a child in the late 60s). Later in the 1980s as 'Monty the Moron' he released albums of songs and pieces on underground cassette label 'Acid Tapes'. This was a period of unemployment, (the Thatcher years) and Monty spent a lot of the time he had on his hands reading in world literature, philosophy and religion. This interest persisted when on long tours in later years.

Apart from a few 'gigs' in front rooms with Acid Folk band 'The Second Attic' he didn't play live until after being encouraged in a letter by Kate Bush (he sent her a tape of his music) he discovered the unique and adventurous cabaret scene at 'The Zap Club' and it was there that he met Captain Sensible. This was exciting for Monty as he was also a fan of the Damned and of Captain's solo albums. It was also during the mid to late 1980s he was undertaking Psychiatric Nurse training based at the big old asylum of Graylingwell in Chichester. The nurse education department shared the library with all sorts of other courses and the library was full of the sort of books Monty was into including the Collected Works of C.G. Jung: a big influence.

Later tutor Rod Paton and students on the 'Related Arts' course persuaded Monty to enrol for the B.A. and this was a great idea as it was a playground after full time work. The course explored all the arts though the lenses of Romanticism, Modernism and Post-

Modernism. Monty incorporated his interest in Sufism and the Gnostics into the course: his dissertation compared the Gnosis of Rumi and William Blake. Also at this time Monty attended several workshops run by Daevid Allen of Gong near Glastonbury (of whom Monty was also a fan.)

In the early 1990s, Having become interested in the Arts Therapies, Monty undertook the Art Psychotherapy course at Goldsmith's College London and though he qualified this did not lead to work, but it did open up avenues into what D.W. Winnicott calls 'the True Self', which in Monty's case is a performing self. He found himself now playing drums, and later keyboards in 'The Doctor Space Toad Experience' (Captain Sensible was playing bass guitar in that most eccentric English Psychedelic band.) After also playing in Captain's 'Punk Floyd' in 1996 he followed the good Captain into a new line-up of one of his favourite bands: the Damned!

Since then Monty evolved 'from stupidity to absurdity' into 'Monty Oxymoron' (the 'moron' epithet being a little too silly even for the Damned), and he toured with them all over the world. Monty Oxymoron performed and wrote on three albums: 'Grave Disorder' (2001), 'So Who's Paranoid?' (2008), and 'Evil Spirits' (2018) and on two DVDs. The latest offering form the band is the EP: 'The Rockfield Files' (2019), which got to number one for a while.

Monty is also an improvising musician in classical, jazz and experimental styles and he is a regular attending member of Brighton's 'Safehouse Collective', a unique evening where player's names are pulled out of a hat and they spontaneously compose pieces together in the moment. Monty plays in the 'Vitamin B12' attic sessions on Sunday afternoons (the 'third attic') He also grooves with psychedelic jazzers 'The Sumerian Kyngs' (sic), and plays solo. In 2019 he played solo piano compositions and improvisations at San Francisco's 'Flower Piano' event in the botanical gardens of the Golden Gate Park (some of this appears on You-Tube.) He also played some solo gigs on the East coast of the US that year.

As Covid 19 has, for now sadly put a stop to all this activity Monty (or Laurence in this case) put his energies into sharing his knowledge of Emotional Intelligence, neurology and Person Centred Care at the nursing home he works at for people with dementia. He still plays music and creates art in his bedroom (just like he did in the 1970s and '80s!) Watch this space...

www.montyoxymoron.com

Printed in Great Britain
by Amazon